Through the Windows of Paris

fifty unique shops

PHOTOGRAPHS AND TEXT BY MICHAEL WEBB

Published in the United States of America 1999

Design by Gretchen Citrin/The Citrin Workshop
Imaging and printing by Navigator Press, Pasadena, California
Printed in USA

THROUGH THE WINDOWS OF PARIS
Fifty Unique Shops

Library of Congress Catalog Card Number: 98-073723
ISBN 1-890449-02-4

Through the Windows of Paris

fifty unique shops

This book was born on the rear platform of a number 29 bus, barreling down the Rue des Francs-Bourgeois in the Marais. Its route, from the Gare St Lazare to the Bastille and beyond, is tortuous, so the driver is usually running behind schedule and puts on speed along this straight stretch. It was evening, and each shop window we passed suggested a miniature theater: its stage decor brightly lit, its mannequins like actors in frozen poses. We, the audience, were rushing by, and I wanted to get off and admire each tableau. But the shops were closed, and it was the last night of my stay in Paris. So I returned the following year, to admire the beauty of carved and painted proscenium arches, the play of light and reflections off the glass, and the abundant surprises backstage.

Above: Aux Tortues,
55 Blvd. Haussmann, 8th
Left: Galérie Perrin,
3 Quai Voltaire, 7th
Right top: Rouge et Noir,
26 Rue Vanvin, 6th
Right below: Lescot Apothicaire
(Musée Carnavalet)

I have always admired the French genius for composition. You can see it in the way women dress and in the arrangement of fruit on a market stall. They are skilled in the art of doing simple things well; they love fantasy and tradition, craft and style. Defiantly individualistic, they have held the franchise tide at bay, preferring to sell a few choice items to a handful of dedicated customers. It can seldom be profitable, but it could be rewarding, and it certainly beats working for a chain.

It is a tradition with deep roots. Frances Trollope, a sharp-eyed Englishwoman whose powers of observation would flower in the novels of her son, Anthony, wrote from Paris in 1835:

"There is an elegance of taste and love of the graceful about these people which is certainly to be found nowhere else...The manner in which an old barrow-woman will tie up cherries for her urchin customers might give a lesson to the most skillful decorator of the supper table...There is a fitness, a propriety, a sort of harmony in the various articles which constitute female attire, which may be traced as clearly amongst the cotton *toques,* with all their variety of brilliant tints, and the 'kerchief and apron to match, or rather to accord, as amongst the most elegant bonnets at the Tuileries." Yet Mrs Trollope was no besotted francophile, for she also wrote that "in a city where the shops and coffee-houses have the air of fairy palaces. . .where the women look too delicate to belong wholly to earth...you are shocked and disgusted at every step you take...by sights and smells that may not be described."

Extremes of elegance and squalor coexisted in early-19th-century Paris, just as they had in the palace of Versailles. As a result, merchants put themselves out to lure strollers from unpaved, unsanitary streets. Boutiques emerged as a civilized alternative to artisanal workshops in which the customer was an intrusion, and they became intimate meeting places for the owner and his clientele. The new rich demanded the latest fashions and luxury goods that were once reserved for the nobility. The great department store, which Emile Zola described so minutely in his novel, *Au Bonheur des Dames,* flattered and seduced the women who were drawn to its vast dis-

Top: Echelle 43.87, 16 Rue de Vangirard, 6th
Bottom: Branly, 9 Rue des Lombards, 4th

plays, setting a standard of service that small shop-keepers had to match.

Paris was transformed from 1852 on, as the Emperor Napoleon III commissioned Baron Haussmann to drive tree-shaded boulevards through medieval labyrinths, spurring new development; speeding traffic, and fostering civic pride. As urban historian Donald J. Olsen observed, the capital became a meticulously regulated

work of art. It has been spared the devastation of war and uncontrolled development, and it has banished its high-rise commercial center to La Défense, beyond the periphery. In its respect for the urban fabric, Paris has changed less than any other great city in the past century, and it is expensively maintained. The density of its population and the diffusion of wealth foster a demand for show among the crowds that throng the sidewalks of every quarter. In London and Milan, the best things are often hidden away; in Paris they are proudly displayed.

Left: Tripéries on the rue Dr. Blanche, 16th, and 178 Rue de la Convention, 15th   Above: Horse butcher turned clothes boutique, 15 Rue Vieille-du-Temple, 4th

Most visitors are awed and exhausted by the monuments and grand vistas, but Parisians enjoy the intimate scale of everyday life. Cramped interiors and the crowded shelves of small shops heighten their allure. The goods crowd in on you, flaunting their textures, aromas, and forms, and engaging all the senses. Parisians are still willing to make the effort and pay the price for quality and personal service. Some find it convenient to purchase their food at a supermarket, but a surprising number still buy bread, cheese, charcuterie, and produce from specialists who do one thing well, and they demand it fresh every day. The same discriminating demand is applied to fashion accessories and collectibles, tableware and picture frames, fine paper and preserved flowers.

As neighborhoods and customs change, some trades decline and are swallowed up by others. The *crémérie-laitérie* that daily sold ice, fresh milk and cream to households without refrigeration has gone, though its north-facing windows, marble slabs and cool cellars are equally appealing to the sellers of cheese. Horse butchers and *tripéries* have become extinct, and there are dozens of vintage bakeries and fishmongers whose ornate facades now frame trendy

Gilded shop-fronts on the Rue Cler, 7th (top) and the Blvd. St-Germain, 5th

clothing. The artisans who created glass paintings of mills and milkmaids in gilded cartouches have died out, but their artistry is valued more than ever. Family ownership is ending in the face of economic pressures and the restlessness of the young. And yet there are exceptions: a teenager insisted her father buy A la Mère de Famille, a confectioner that was founded in 1761 and is now likely to provide another century of delight.

Ladurée, 16 Rue Royale, 8th

You, dear reader, probably love to shop. I confess I used to regard it as a disagreeable chore, and I entered these boutiques in mortal fear that I should make some extravagant purchase or be thrown out for merely browsing. Instead, I was welcomed and invited to linger and chat. Most of the owners I met felt they were performing a labor of love. They cared passionately about the authenticity of what they sold, and were eager to tell me how it was made or where they had found it. My French improved dramatically, and I felt I was enjoying free lessons in French civilization. The one unpleasant experience in a month of showing up unannounced with my camera was at Ladurée, the tea room-*patisserie* on the Rue Royale. A white-coated member of the staff ran towards me, accusing me of sneaking a picture from the sidewalk and—discovering I was born in England—screamed *"vache folle! vache folle!"* (mad cow! mad cow!). It seemed a small annoyance amid so many rewarding encounters.

Corinne Guisez, Linda de Nazelle and Marie-Claude Béaud helped me find shops that had a distinct personality, and did things that weren't replicated around the world. To them and for the encouragement of many friends in Paris, my deep appreciation. Reluctantly I omitted some legendary names. Hermès, Vuitton and the *haute couture* are decidedly French, but they have become multi-national corporations that sell the same goods in the same manner, from

Above: Toy shops at 31 Rue Roi-de-Sicile, 4th (top) and 68 Galérie Vivienne, 2nd   Right top: Guillon Fleurs, 120 Blvd. Raspail, 6th Right below: Le Bonheur de Dames, 8 Passage Verdeau, 9th

London to Tokyo. However, I have included a few traditional shops that have expanded or opened local branches without compromising their character. I looked for emporia that had been around for a long time—355 years in one case—or which had recently decided to buck the trend towards profitability by embracing some eccentric specialty. They are grouped thematically, as you can see from the list of addresses in back, though several belong in more than one category.

This celebration of fifty remarkable shops includes necessities, luxuries, and frivolities. Appropriately it begins with the most essential amenity of daily life—bakeries. A cry for bread helped ignite the French Revolution, and a homeward-bound Parisian feels incomplete without a baguette tucked under his arm (though the mobile telephone seems to be taking its place). Relays of fresh loaves satisfy the craving from dawn till dusk, and you can pick up the aromas in every neighborhood. Traditional brioches, croissants, and *pain de campagne* sit side by side with whimsical variations on classic themes.

Poilâne on the Rue du Cherche-Midi is a shrine to the art of baking—from the pyramid of crusty rounds in the window to the bread chandelier that lights an inner room hung with paintings of loaves. Below is a 12th-century cellar, where, in motions as rhythmic and graceful as those of a gondolier, a young man scatters flour onto a long wooden paddle, dumps two baskets of dough onto the blade, adds ornament and slides it into the wood-fired oven, repeating the action until there are 40 loaves rising in the heat. These will satisfy the neighbors, but Poilâne also supplies its distinctive sourdough to shops and restaurants all over the city and by air to New York and Tokyo, drawing on 24 traditional ovens in a model plant on the outskirts of Paris. Presiding over this empire is Lionel, son of Pierre who opened this shop in 1933: a shrewd businessman and something of a dandy, with long hair and a taste for floppy bow ties. (Lionel has a brother, Max, whose historic bakery at 87 Rue Brancion, in the 15th, is well worth a visit).

POILAN

Jean-Luc Poujauran still has the earthiness of a country boy who grew up in a village near Bordeaux where his father was a baker, and served a 14-year apprenticeship before coming to Paris in 1976 and taking over a century-old bakery with a painted glass ceiling. In contrast to the dapper M. Poilâne, who may be seen holding court at a local café, Poujauran is a hands-on boss who cuts the cookies for a special order and help out behind the counter when the line gets too long. Specialties of southwestern France crowd the racks: chewy country bread with hazel nuts and raisins, brioches with orange flowers, and canélés—which resemble a tiny rum baba. Everything is made in house, and the hard-pressed owner is hoping to expand his kitchen without sacrificing the intimacy of his shop.

POUJAURAN

The rum baba was invented by M. Stohrer, pastry chef to King Stanislas of Poland. In 1725, when the king's daughter, Marie Leszynska, married Louis XV of France, Stohrer accompanied her to Versailles. Five years later he opened the *patissérie* that still bears his name on the Rue Montorgueil, a market street near Les Halles. The painted and mirrored interior, with its gauzy nymphs bearing garlands and cakes, is as glorious a memento of the 1860s as the lobby of the Opera Garnier—and was done by the same artist, Paul Baudry. Tradition is currently upheld by Pierre Liénard and François Duthu, who will sell you a single *puits d'amour* (well of love) and a bag of *financières* to nibble with your coffee, or will cater the grandest of parties.

STOHRER

51 Rue Montorgueil, 2nd; 42 33 38 20 (daily 7.30am-8.30pm

HÉDIARD

Hédiard is a cluster of specialized boutiques under one roof—and a lot friendlier than Fauchon, a rival temple of gastronomy on the opposite side of Place Madeleine. Founded by Ferdinand Hédiard in 1854, it introduced Parisians to exotic spices and produce, sold from open stalls by pretty young women from the Caribbean island of Martinique. Colette and Chaplin, Jean Cocteau and Marlene Dietrich shopped here. The store was remodeled in 1994, and is now the flagship of an enterprise that makes or imports 6000 items, has added several branches in Paris and is eyeing the rest of the world. But the traditional character remains in the lofty atrium, with its steel beams, exotic woods, and tiled floor, and in its artful displays. The open sacks of coffee beans, red-lacquered canisters of teas, and aromatic hillocks of fresh-ground spices feel as accessible as in a street market. Trays of the freshest fruits and vegetables are propped up on barrels and stenciled wooden boxes, with chile peppers looped above like Christmas lights. The staff encourage browsing, and the upstairs restaurant is open early for breakfast and late for supper.

HEDIARD

21 Place de la Madeleine, 8th; 43 12 88 88   (Mo-Sa 9.15am-10pm)

"Papa, you must buy A la Merè de Famille," insisted Serge Neveu's daughter, afraid that the vintage confectioner where she had lingered as a child would succumb to progress. Father came through, making his family the staff of an enterprise that began in 1761 when the bustling Rue du Faubourg-Montmartre was still a country lane. During the French Revolution, a nun took refuge in its cellars and gave her protector a recipe for eye lotion, which was added to the varied stock. Today the emphasis is more on home-made chocolates than ingredients for plum pudding, but little else seems to have changed in the past century. The facade is richly ornamented with gold lettering proclaiming long-forgotten brands and specialties, and products fill the expansive windows so that the light filters in through jars of preserves and colored liqueurs. The cashier sits on a glass-enclosed throne, and it's easy to imagine a line of women in stiff bustled dresses lining up to pay their bills.

A LA MERE DE FAMILLE

35 Rue du Faubourg-Montmartre, 9th; 47 70 83 69   (Tu-Sa 9.30am-1.30pm, 3-7pm

President de Gaulle despaired of governing a country that produced over 200 cheeses, but your only problem is to make a good selection. That's easy to do at Barthélémy, a *fromagérie* on the chic Rue de Grenelle, whose customers include Catherine Deneuve and the Elysée Palace. A tiled facade the color of ripe Camembert is flanked by a vintage glass panel painted with rustic scenes; baskets and cow creamers play supporting roles in the window. Within, white coated assistants take your order in a room that's as clean and cool as a dairy (which it once was), but full of delicious aromas from the cheeses that line the walls and sit out on marble counters. Here you can travel through France from the meadows of Normandy to the rugged terrain of Corsica, and find everything in perfect condition. Roland Barthélémy's parents ran a cheese shop in the Jura, and he is now a master of his profession and head of its guild. He stalks his cellars like a beagle on the scent, while explaining that cheeses engage all the senses.

BARTHELEMY

51 Rue de Grenelle, 7th; 45 48 56 75   (Tu-Sa 8.30am-1pm; 3.30-7.15pm

In 1800, Sulpice Débauve, pharmacist and chocolate maker to Louis XVI, had recently lost his employer to the guillotine. So he joined with his nephew to found Débauve et Gallais on the Rue des Saintes-Pères, combining his interests in health and indulgence. He commissioned an Empire-style facade and interior from Percier and Fontaine, architects of Malmaison and the Carrousel Arch, and attracted a distinguished clientele. The gourmand Brillat-Savarin praised the restorative quality of orange and vanilla-flavored chocolates, and the soothing *pastilles de la reine* that were a favorite of Marie Antoinette. Balzac and Proust shared his enthusiasm, as have a two-centuries parade of choca-holics who are delighted to learn that such sinfully delicious treats can also do them good. Extravagant Easter eggs are a major attraction, and the shop has two stylish branches.

DEBAUVE ET GALLAIS

30 Rue des Saintes-Pères, 7th; 45 48 54 67   (Tu-Sa 10am-7pm

Suave young men in ecru linen suits measure out teas that can cost as much as $21 an ounce at the ancient emporium of Mariage Frères in the Marais. There are 450 to choose from, and the sales assistants will give you a tour of Asia and beyond in your search for the perfect wake-up or nightcap. Painted canisters with gold lettering and an upstairs museum evoke the firm's history as importers of tea, beginning with the East India trade in the 18th century. The retail operation began in the 1980s, when this aromatic depot was converted into a shop and a colonial-style tea room, serving a variety of pastries and tea-flavored dishes and provoking your interest in a range of accessories with which to make the perfect brew. There are branches in the Latin Quarter and on the Faubourg Saint-Honoré, plus six in Japan.

MARIAGE FRERES

30-32 Rue du Bourg-Tibourg, 4th; 42 72 28 11 (Tu-Su 10am-7.30pm

Few wine merchants have more atmosphere and a richer stock than Legrand Fille et Fils. Behind the glossy red Belle Epoque facade with its stately gold lettering is a ceiling covered with corks—inviting buyers to add to the collection. There are bottles at every price, the legendary labels mixed in with young and unfamiliar wines, selected by Francine Legrand-Richard, and a good selection of groceries. A spiral stair descends as precipitously as a firemen's pole from the upstairs office. Walk around the corner from the Rue de la Banque and into the elegant Galérie Vivienne, and you'll discover the back window of Legrand, which displays corkscrews and other accessories.

LEGRAND FILLE ET FILS

1 Rue de la Banque, 2nd 42 60 07 12   (Tu-Fr 8.30am-7pm; Sa 8.30am-1pm, 3-7pm)

Late-19th-century dolls are the specialty of Robert Capia, a 40-year occupant of three arched store fronts in the Galerie Véro-Dodat, a once-fashionable, now shabby arcade of 1826 that is located between the Palais-Royal and the Bourse du Commerce. To protect his treasures from the idly curious, he has half-hidden them in an obstacle course of antiques and bric-a-brac. If you can reach his desk without knocking something fragile off its perch and manifest sufficient enthusiasm, he will show you, first some commonplace dolls, and then, if you have the air of a true collector, beauties from the Golden Age, 1870-99. As the author of definitive books on this subject, he can tell you who made them, where and when (typically, one of ten masters working in Les Halles or the Marais) and, in contrast to his clockwork automata, it's hard to stop him when he's fully wound up.

ROBERT CAPIA

24-26 Galerie Véro-Dodat, 1st; 42 36 25 94   (Mo-Sa 10am-7pm)

La Maison de Poupée, across from the Luxembourg Gardens, is the creation of Françoise du Rot Hazard, who followed her mother's example in collecting dolls from an early age, and started selling them in this old grocery in 1979. She welcomes browsers, and a languid tone is set by the cat snoozing in an open drawer. There are French porcelain antiques, painted wood figures from Germany, and wax dolls from Britain, along with paintings, puppet theaters, and creches. Disembodied heads and arms indicate that a restoration is in progress. Everything is in plain view, lovingly arranged, and the window display is especially inviting.

LA MAISON DE POUPEE

40 Rue de Vaugirard, 6th; 46 33 74 05   (Mo-Sa 2.30-7pm

23, RUE DE BEAUNE
75007 PARIS
TEL/FAX, 01 42 61 09 57
06 03 03 38 94

At the heart of the Carré Rive Gauche, seven blocks of antique stores across the Seine from the Louvre, is Le Cabinet de Curiosité, which occupies a former pharmacy of 1804. The shop is aptly named, for Claudine Guerin has an eye for the odd, juxtaposing a model staircase that an apprentice carpenter carved from walnut as his masterpiece with a wire mannequin of the 1940s, and placing a threatening set of teeth across from an 18th-century portrait of a dwarf. Elegant columns, a painted frieze, and other fragments of the original decor pull these disparate objects together in a surreal, yet balanced tableau.

LE CABINET DE CURIOSITE
23 Rue de la Beaune, 7th; 42 61 09 57   (Mo-Sa 11am-7pm

"I was an actor in the provinces, playing everything from Molière to musical comedy—even a transvestite," declares M-G. Segas with a theatrical wave. He accumulated a few sticks as props, then got the bug, and has spent the past 25 years buying and selling antiques from his shop in the Passage Jouffroy. Moose antlers branching from his facade and the carved heads on his stock belong to the world of fantasy, and it's appropriate that he should be a neighbor of the Musée Grévin, where the celebrated and notorious are modeled in wax. Downstairs, red velvet curtains and gilded arches evoke the stage; upstairs he displays his private collection to fellow enthusiasts.

LA GALERIE 34

34 Passage Jouffroy, 9th; 47 70 89 65   (Mo-Sa 11.30am-6.30pm)

L'HERMINETTE

Old tools and rustic antiques are the stock-in-trade of L'Herminette, one of 240 boutiques that are housed in Le Louvre des Antiquaires, the former Grand Hôtel du Louvre, where Mark Twain lodged in 1867. In contrast to the pampered perfection of neighboring displays, Christine Leblic has created atmospheric still-lifes of weathered iron and wood, decoys and weather vanes, 19th-century hinges and keys, set off by a lace curtain. On a wet day, this Louvre rivals the art museum as a place to browse. However, there's no admission charge and you can buy and carry home whatever grabs your fancy.

L'HERMINETTE

At the end of a cobbled alley leading off the Rue de Seine are rooms crammed with majolica birds and flowers, set off by garden furniture and framed by trellis. Au Fond de la Cour conjures up an eccentric country house, in which elderly aunts with sharp eyes and deep pockets have assembled a lifetime of acquisitions. Taken as a whole, Marie-Laure de l'Ecotais' treasury is too much of a good thing, but one of her antique flamingos or parrots might be just the thing to give your home a lift.

AU FOND DE LA COUR

49 Rue de Seine, 6th; 43 25 81 89   (Mo-Sa 11am-7pm,

Madeleine Gély is an ebullient, gray-haired sprite who can tell you the history of every one of the umbrellas and walking sticks that are crammed into her tiny shop, while jealously guarding the identities of her skilled artisans. There's a menagerie of animal-head handles from the mountains of the Auvergne, where villagers spend long winter nights carving hares and foxes from wood and horn. Umbrellas are suspended from a ceiling that resembles a giant parasol. Everything here is made in France, though often from exotic materials, and there was even a scarlet special with a football handle to celebrate the World Cup. Two's a crowd inside, so you may have to step outside to open an umbrella or swing a cane. But the quality is guaranteed: this firm has been in business since 1834.

MADELEINE GELY

218 Blvd St-Germain, 7th; 42 22 63 35 (Tu-Su 9.30am-7pm,

The porticoes of the Palais-Royal and the succession of 19th-century shopping arcades extending north are a paradise for collectors. There is something for every taste and budget, from rare books to marble fruit, comics to clocks. At Les Drapeaux de la France you could impersonate Napoleon and re-fight his greatest battles, deploying brigades of painted lead soldiers that thrust and parry and flaunt their banners. Whole armies are stacked on glass shelves to the full height of the windows and you can choose your favorite period, from medieval to modern—though the 18th century is clearly the winner. Some of these tiny figures are imported, most were made in France, and all have been painted by experts to assure authenticity of costumes and equipment. The shop was established in 1950 and has expanded into six spaces, looking out through the arches and iron railings to the formal gardens of the Palais-Royal.

LES DRAPEAUX DE LA FRANCE

34, 37-38 Galérie Montpensier, 1st; 40 20 00 11   (Mo-Sa 10am-7pm)

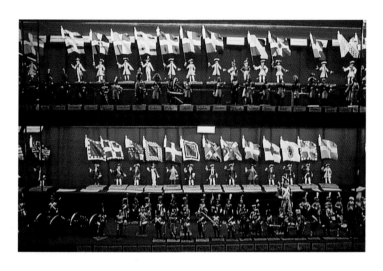

Located a few doors away from the model army, A Marie-Stuart boasts it can provide every medal in the world, and it claims to be the oldest shop of its kind in France. It was founded 200 years ago by a jeweler who specialized in the black gemstones that were worn by ladies in mourning, and he dedicated his shop to a queen who was thrice widowed. A mid-19th-century owner switched to decorations, and the windows now resemble the chests of military heroes, ablaze with gongs and striped silk ribbons. Many more are concealed in drawers, awaiting an order from a mayor or minister, but you are allowed to award yourself a prize for your own collection.

A MARIE-STUART

3-5 Galérie Montpensier, 1st; 42 96 28 25 *(Mo-Fr 9am-6.30pm; Sa 9am-noon; 2-6pm)*

Sunlight filters through the glass vault of the languid Passage Jouffroy giving it an aqueous quality—a perfect setting for Thomas Boog's shell-encrusted urns, lamps and furniture. Born in the mountains of Switzerland, he felt drawn to the sea-shore and there developed a passion for the natural colors and shapes of shells. He abandoned shoe design to revive a craft that flourished in classical times and the age of enlightenment before declining into kitsch. Boog insists that he is an artisan, producing useful objects, but everything he does is infused by a sense of fantasy, and his love of *chinoiserie* finds expression in dragon handles and swelling shades. Over the past decade, he has

transformed his back room into a grotto, with a shell chandelier highlighting the boldly patterned walls and vault, and he'll be happy to make one for you.

THOMAS BOOG

36 Passage Jouffroy, 9th; 47 70 98 10   (Mo-Sa 1-7pm

Behind the Bastille Opera is an old brick railroad viaduct that has been transformed into the Viaduc des Arts, with shops in the arches and a half mile of landscaped promenade where the tracks once ran. It resembles an outdoor arcade, and has attracted a lively mix of craft-related enterprises, from hunting horns to architectural models. Cabinetmaker Jérôme Cordié has opened Aisthesis, where he makes and restores inlaid furniture. The tools of his trade are displayed as though they were objects of art and to demonstrate his commitment to tradition. Cordié will sketch a unique piece, inlaid with mother of pearl, perhaps, or covered in shagreen, which will become an heirloom of tomorrow.

AISTHESIS

25 Avenue Daumesnil, 12th; 53 33 00 45 (Mo-Sa 9am-1pm, 2-6pm; Su 2-6pm

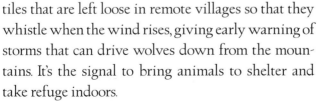

Marie-France and Michel Joblin-Dépalle came to Paris from the Auvergne in central France, and opened La Tuile à Loup in 1974. Traditional crafts were dying out, and the couple wanted to support the best artisans of all 16 regions of France by creating a showcase for their work. Everything in their joyously exuberant shop is made by hand and was chosen for its utility and artistry on their buying trips around the country. Every square centimeter of shelving is piled high with platters and casseroles, baskets and glasses, pigs and hens in treacly glazes, and soft wool blankets. There's a full library of books on rural traditions, stories, and ethnography; in brief, the country has come to town. Even the name of the shop is significant; *tuiles à loup* are roof

tiles that are left loose in remote villages so that they whistle when the wind rises, giving early warning of storms that can drive wolves down from the mountains. It's the signal to bring animals to shelter and take refuge indoors.

LA TUILE A LOUF

🏛 *Palladio*

Italian glass by masters old and new is the principal theme at Palladio, a jeweled cave on a street that's full of treasures. Doriane and Denis Brill launched the enterprise in 1995 after spending a month selecting from the best of Florence and Murano, then adding golden carnival masks from Venice and objects carved from Carrara marble. Lacy chandeliers add sparkle to an interior that seems to glow from within, in tones of ruby and emerald, sapphire and topaz. Carlo Moretti and other modern masters are well represented, alongside stylish trifles that are quintessentially Italian.

PALLADIO

27 Rue des Saintes-Pères, 6th; 40 15 09 15   *(Mo 2.30-7pm; Tu-Sa 10.30-7pm)*

Entrée des Artistes translates as "stage door" but it is also the title of a French film of the 1930s that starred Louis Jouvet, a great actor who lends his brooding presence to the facade. Both references are apt, for owner Philippe Dubuc specializes in vintage movie posters, books and stills (though Leonardo di Caprio and other contemporary hearthrobs have crept in when he wasn't looking). Marionettes and *commedia dell'arte* masks are suspended above antique music boxes and automata. Dubuc took over a former café in 1985; earlier, the shop sold suitings when this was a clothing district and Les Halles was the belly of Paris. Around the corner is the Passage Molière, where the playwright gave a reading of *Tartuffe,* in defiance of a ban on performance.

ENTREE DES ARTISTES
161 Rue St Martin, 3rd; 48 87 78 58   (Mo-Sa 11am-7.30pm

Roberta Rivin is an American in Paris, and the Galérie Urubamba is her showcase of the traditional arts of indigenous American peoples, from the Yukon to Tierra del Fuego. Having lived in Brazil and studied anthropology, she decided to fill in a blank on the French cultural map of the world, and took over an ancient butcher's shop in a leafy square beside the Seine. Over the past 25 years, she has added books, tribal regalia, and embroidered garments, luring a clientele that ranges from punks to full-blood Indians from north and south of the Rio Grande. She organizes seminars and her shop—a listed property of the 17th century that retains the old meat hooks and oak beams—has become a lively little museum.

GALERIE URUBAMBA

4 Rue de la Buchérie, 5th; 43 54 08 24   (Tu-Sa 2-7.30pm,

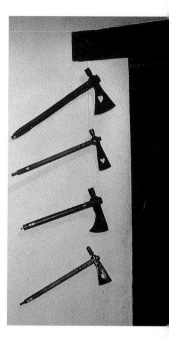

The closing of Les Halles spelt ruin to hundreds of small businesses, and Papetérie Moderne might easily have been a casualty. Joseph Bakerdjian took over a former barber shop in 1967, and made a specialty of waxed wrapping paper, bags, and price tags. Six years later, when the market moved to the suburbs, he had the inspired idea of adding enameled signs to his stock, and these have now taken over the tiny storefront. You no longer have to risk a fine or worse while unscrewing a sign to take home as a souvenir of Paris. Rue des Mauvais-Garçons or Place de la Concorde can be yours, wrapped and shipped to your door. Authentic name plates of favorite streets that are not in stock can be made to order. You can identify your pet as a *chien bizarre* or a *chat méchant*, proclaim your profession, or discourage people from spitting—provided they have a good command of French.

PAPETERIE MODERNE

12 Rue de la Ferronérie, 1st; 42 36 21 72   (Mo-Sa 9am-noon, 1-8pm)

The Passage des Panoramas is 200 years old and has seen better days, but Stern seems not to have changed since it moved here in 1840. Faux marble columns frame displays of engraved invitations, menus, and writing paper of a quality and restraint that Proust would have treasured. Stern is in every way a survivor. It is one of the last engravers in Paris, and its customers are received in one of four ornate rooms, where they may place their orders at leather-covered tables. The atmosphere is that of an immensely dignified town house, with parquet floors, barley-sugar columns in dark shiny wood, and wallpaper that resembles tooled leather. If you've ever wanted a book plate that will shame friends into returning what they borrow, or a calling card that will impress strangers, you've found the best source.

STERN

47 Passage des Panoramas, 2nd; 45 08 86 45   *(Mo-Fr 9.30am-12.30pm, 1.30-5.30pm)*

The Quartier Latin is book city, with an emphasis on deep thinking, so it's a relief to find a shop that is—in the best sense—escapist. The owner's powerful motor bike is propped in front of the Librairie Monte Cristo and the window is full of mementos of travel. A brass telescope, a globe, and a model of the Nautilus from *20,000 Leagues Under the Sea*, top a display of Jules Verne in gilded 19th-century editions. Verne is the star attraction, but there's a wide choice of illustrated adventures, travelers' tales and vintage children's books. You wish this were a library with a comfortable chair in which you could drift off on imaginary voyages.

LIBRAIRIE MONTE CRISTO

5 Rue de l'Odéon, 6th; 43 26 49 03   (Tu-Sa 11am-1pm, 2.30-7pm,

One of the grandest *boucheries* in Paris, with a patterned marble facade and carved wood frames, has become a wonderfully ramshackle bookshop that specializes in literature of every kind. Established in 1974 by the poet Marcel Béalu, it is now run by his widow, Josée. Ceiling hooks recall the sides of beef and lamb that must once have occupied the space; now the challenge is to step lightly around tottering piles and climb the ladder past laden shelves, hoping they won't come crashing down as you search for an elusive volume of Baudelaire's poetry or a nice copy of Antoine de St Exupéry's *Le Petit Prince*.

LE PONT TRAVERSEE

62 Rue de Vaugirard, 6e; 45 48 06 48   (Tu-Sa noon-7pm

Do you love bold colors? Marie-Paule Orluc does, and she has installed her boutique, Marie Papier, in the ground floor of a terraced apartment block, designed by Henri Sauvage in 1912. This is one of the earliest and most appealing modern buildings in Paris, and its white tiled facade provides the perfect overture to a rainbow of wrapping and writing papers, pencils and notebooks, stacked methodically in boxes and draped from rails. You don't need to write a letter: a scarlet sheet in a turquoise envelope will send its own message of good cheer. A patterned mosaic floor adds another layer to this visual extravaganza. As you walk away, with colors imprinted on your retinas, the exterior seems even whiter than before.

MARIE PAPIER

26 Rue Vavin, 6th; 43 26 46 44   (Mo-Sa 10am-7pm)

It's too bad that Dîners en Ville doesn't offer a catering service, for you could happily group your friends around one of their elegantly arranged tables and tuck in. Colors conspire to whet the appetite: the burgundy of the facade is brought inside in the carpet and display cabinets and set off by ochre yellow walls. Flatware handles in sorbet hues are set out on a table cloth that is as boldly printed as a Hermès scarf. Italian faience and Portuguese copies of 19th-century Baccarat lusterware are set off by eye-deceiving plastic fruit. Tiny potted trees, an *étagère* stacked with

shells, and cabbage-leaf bowls add notes of whimsy. It's all good enough to eat, thanks to the audacious taste of proprietor Blandine de Mandat-Grancey, who opened her emporium in 1980.

DINERS EN VILLE
27 Rue deVarenne, 7th; 42 22 78 33   (Mo 2-7pm; Tu-Sa 11am-7pm)

A villa in Morocco inspired Bertrand Massé and Myriam Goldmann to create the Villa Marais in 1994, and the warm-toned plaster and pale blue ceiling beams set off an eclectic mix of antiques, custom furnishings and straw hats. He was formerly in communications, she in catering, but their passion for architecture and design, preferably *un peu fou*, persuaded them to gamble on marketing another kind of taste. Designers arrived with portfolios

and left with commissions; Massé designed many of the pieces himself, trying to offer good value and originality—a rare combination.

VILLA MARAIS
40 Rue des Francs-Bourgeois, 3rd; 42 78 42 40   (daily 10.30am-7.30pm)

Don't be put off by the slightly shabby facade of the Maison de Famille. Like a duchess who disdains outward show, this store is the embodiment of quiet good taste. From the expansive windows, through a succession of rooms, and up to the attic, the goods are stacked on tables and arranged on racks with artless simplicity. They speak for themselves. This is where a well-bred young woman would come to furnish her first home with ivory linen sheets and café-au-lait towels, white bone china and heavy silver flatware. The aristocratic character of the Faubourg St Germain is evidenced here, in Catherine Memmi across the street, and in the showroom of Christian Liaigre, the French master of zen, on the Rue du Bac.

MAISON DE FAMILLE

29 Rue St Sulpice, 6th; 40 46 97 47 (Mo 2.30-7.30pm; Tu-Sa 10.30am-7.30pm,

Straddling the end of a passage that leads out of Place Madeleine is Territoire, which describes itself as a *magasin général*—a French version of the American general store. Its logo—a 17th-century engraving of a man armored in kitchenware—is a nod to the hardware shop that once occupied these handsome premises, and to the weird diversity of its current stock. It offers things you had never thought you wanted—Swiss dog collars, embroidered Spanish waistcoats, and a model yacht you could sail in the pond of the Luxembourg Gardens. It reminds you of the changing seasons, with picnic sets for summer, a knife and brush for fall mushroom hunters, and Canadian snow shoes for that sudden blizzard. Established in 1988, it belongs in spirit to an earlier, less systematic age.

TERRITOIRE

30 Rue Boissy d'Anglas, 8th; 42 66 22 13 (daily 10.30am-7pm,

Cir was founded in 1643, the year Louis XIV ascended the throne, and they still sell the candle they made for the Sun King, aptly named the *bougie royale*. Their present shop is new, and is doubtful that the kings of France would recognize candles disguised as cream pastries, ducks and penguins. Basic candles are available in 36 eye-popping colors, but the window display sticks to basics: white altar candles and tapers, which they supply to the great church of St Sulpice across the street.

22 Rue St Sulpice, 6th; 43 26 46 50   (Mo 11am-7pm; Tu-Sa 10am-7pm)

For a crash course in opening a restaurant, you should watch the staff of Déhillerin (a family-run business since 1820) making up an order. The patron checks off the list as three assistants retrieve a *battérie de cuisine* from the brimming shelves, assembling a pile of whisks and ladles, pans and casseroles, racks and lids, each numbered by size. Within minutes, everything has been wrapped, packed into taped boxes, and stacked for dispatch. Looking around, you imagine they could replenish half the kitchens of Paris without exhausting their stock. This is Mecca for chefs and aficionados, who know that the shiniest copper will perform as well as the basic aluminum, and that they will find the latest Robot Coupe alongside a time-tested *moulin.*

DEHILLERIN

18-20 Rue Coquillière, 1st; 42 36 53 13   (Mo-Sa 8am-12.30pm, 2-6pm,

Paris is no longer the world capital of art, but the arts are woven into its fabric, and almost every shop on the Left Bank displays posters for the latest exhibitions. Charbonnel, across the Seine from Notre Dame, has long provided everything artists need. Behind its modest facade are serried rows of brushes and Conté crayons, sketchbooks and paints, palettes and easels extending into back rooms. The plane trees along the quai can be glimpsed through frosted glass windows and the light sparkles off stoppered jars of colored liquid that recall those in an old-fashioned pharmacy.

CHARBONNEL

13 Quai de Montebello, 5th; 43 54 23 46   (Mo & Sa 10am-5pm; Tu-Fr 9.30am-6pm)

Art supply stores and framers are clustered around the Ecole des Beaux-Arts, where young hopefuls dream of emulating the giants who once had studios along the quais—Ingres, Delacroix and Corot among them. Sennélier opened for business in 1887, when the Impressionists were in full flower, and it's been the emporium of choice for generations of celebrated artists and aspirants. Its expansive windows are art works in themselves, and they frame reflections of the Pont du Carrousel which leads across to the Louvre. The business is still owned by the family that began it, providing another link to the past.

SENNELIER

3 Quai Voltaire, 7th; 42 60 72 15   (Mo 9am-noon, 2-6.15pm; Tu-Sa 9am-6.15pm)

Messieurs Renevey and Gault are master framers in the tradition of the craftsmen who extablished Cadres RG in 1935. Past customers included Matisse and Picasso, Utrillo and Chagall, but you are more likely to encounter a collector or dealer today. The ornate gilded frames that are the pride of this firm are based on 18th-century models and are fabricated in a workshop in Burgundy. It has become hard to find artisans who will serve a long apprenticeship in Paris, so craft shops in the capital increasingly reach out to the provinces for the special skills they require.

LES CADRES RG

9 Rue Bonaparte, 6th; 43 26 41 77 (Tu-Sa 9am-noon, 2-6pm)

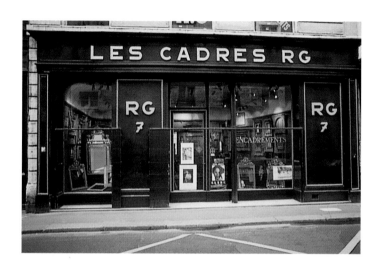

A luthier is a maker of stringed instruments, and guitarist François Perrin and Jean-Paul Bru, who plays the violin, are masters of their craft. For 30 years, violins, cellos and exotica have filled the ground floor of the Hôtel de Savourny in the Marais, and professional musicians gather here to discuss the merits of an acquisition or to drop off a favorite for repair. There's a basement workshop, where classics are refurbished and new instruments made by hand in the traditional way. Chamber concerts are held in the salon upstairs, so that these rooms are alive with the sound of music at all hours.

A BRU ET PERRIN

Luthiers, 4 rue Elzévir, 4th; 42 77 68 42 (Mo-Sa 9.30am-12.30pm, 2.30-6.30pm

The ebullient André Bissonnet comes from a long line of butchers in the Loire, and, after learning his trade, he set up shop just off the Place des Vosges in 1969. Four years later he abruptly switched careers. Out went the meat, in came an extraordinary collection of antique musical instruments, including many rustic oddities. A collector of curiosities since childhood, Bissonnet had taught himself to play the harmonium; now he practiced the hunting horn, hurdy gurdy, and serpent until he could pick out a tune on every instrument in the store. He loaned period viols for *Tous les Matins du Monde,* a feature movie on 17th-century court music, and his knowledge of musical history has become encyclopedic. But his true passions are to replenish his stock (since everything is for sale) and to bring his treasures to life.

ANDRE BISSONNET

6 Rue Pas-de-la-Mule, 3rd; 48 87 20 15 (Mo-Sa 2-7pm)

Butterflies flutter around exquisitely arranged orchids, roses and magnolias. Every bloom is perfect—thanks to the wizardry of Emilio Robba, creator of this grand illusion. The flowers are silk, the butterflies are wired, and the foliage is preserved; even the water in the crystal vases is simulated. Robba, however is quite real. Born in Paris to a family of Italian artists, he studied painting, switched to horticulture, wrought his magic, and now lives in Miami. The Japanese can't get enough of his work, but the place to see it in all its glory is behind the tall arched windows of his shop in the city's most elegant 19th-century arcade, and in the cellars below. You can buy a stem or a bouquet, a vase and a table to set it on.

EMILIO ROBBA

29-33 Galérie Vivienne, 2nd; 42 60 43 46   (Mo-Fr 10.30am-7pm; Sa 11am-7pm)

Les Couturiers de la Nature may be the smallest, newest, and most perfectly composed of all the shops in this collection. In the hands of designer Brigitte Half, dried flowers are turned into exquisite objects and abstract compositions that recall the manicured topiary of French formal gardens and the brilliant colors of a *fauve* canvas. Tiny flowering trees, bouquets and sheaves are set off by walls of preserved leaves. Half has chosen a good name for her enterprise: vegetation is for her what fabric is to a couturier.

LES COUTURIERS DE LA NATURE

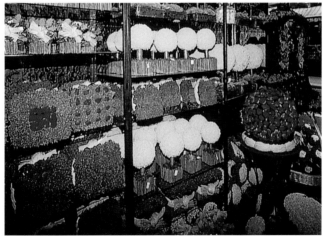

ew tenants of the Viaduc des Arts have employed their arch as imaginatively as Vertical, which has lofted a balloon into the vault and positioned trees to reach up into the space. Alban Lanoré and Nanou Grimault moved their fledgling design business here from a ware-house in the suburbs and the change of scene has boosted their creativity. They import dried cactus from Chile, branches from the California desert, and roots from Africa to sell as natural sculpture, or weave into decor for an office or display window. You can buy a single preserved rose or a nine-foot pine, a mossy folding screen or a chair that resembles a hollow log.

Viaduc des Arts
63 avenue Daumesnil
7 5 0
Tél.: 01 43 40 26 26
Fax : 01

VERTICAL

63 Avenue Daumesnil, 12th; 43 40 26 26   (Mo-Fr 10am-1pm, 2.30-8pm; Sa 11am-1.30pm, 3-8pm,

W aren—she prefers to use only one name—teeters on the divide between artifice and practicality. Her hats, which have graced the runways at major fashion shows, seem as delicate as cobwebs or dandelion seeds, certain to take wing in the lightest of breezes. She describes herself as a *parurière*—practicing the ancient craft of applying ornament—and she shapes her creations from gauze and straw, dried flowers and leaves, working alone, or sending her designs out to be made up by milliners. A sylph-like girl comes in with her mother to pick a hat for a summer wedding. She tries on one, then another, and each heightens her self-confidence and intensifies her allure. The magic has worked again.

WAREN CREATIONS

46 Rue du Roi-de-Sicile, 4th; 42 71 16 06   (Tu, Th, Fr 11.30am-1pm, 2.30-7.30pm; We, Sa 2.30-8pm)

As a little girl, Marie Mercié was intrigued by hats, but she studied archeology and took up painting after graduating from the Sorbonne. Her English husband encouraged her to become a milliner, and she approached it systematically, quizzing veterans and learning the craft, before opening her first shop, a decade ago. Classic, romantic, and inventive by turns, her hats can evoke a prewar garden party or the brilliant ice creams of Berthillon. Recent additions included a straw scallop shell and a top hat of wire mesh. Pleasurable extravagance is her goal, and she keeps eight artisans, each with an individual specialty, fully employed on her seasonal collections.

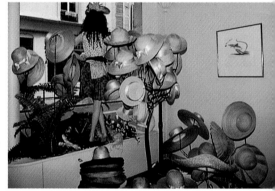

MARIE MERCIE

23 rue St Sulpice, 6th; 43 26 45 83 (Tu-Sa 11am-7pm)

It's a long time since Paris led the world in naughtiness, but there's a faint memory of grand dukes drinking champagne from chorus girls' slippers in the sybaritic lingerie of Sabbia Rosa. She opened her boutique in 1976, and sends her designs out to be hand-made from the finest silks and satins, ribbons and lace, using bold and delicate colors and patterns. One eye-catching creation dominates the elegant vitrine; within, *femmes fatales* and their well-heeled lovers can select from bras, slips and robes that mingle fantasy and tradition.

SABBIA ROSA

1-73 Rue des Saintes-Pères, 6th; 45 48 88 37   (Mo-Sa 10am-7pm)

A la Bonne Renomée is a clothes store that defies the dictates of fashion. In a former industrial loft in the Marais, designers Elisabeth Gratacap and Catherine Legrand deploy dresses and separates on antique mannequins. The styles are curiously timeless—one could be at a party in Soho or in the drawing room of your eccentric grandmother, 50 years ago. The partners complement each other. Elisabeth was a graphic designer and loves sports; Catherine was a professor of design and is inspired by other cultures. The product of their collaboration is artistic, eclectic, and unlikely to go out of style.

A LA BONNE RENOMEE

26 Rue Vieille du Temple, 4th; 42 72 03 86   (Mo-Sa 11am-7pm)

It must be fun to grow up in Paris, where children are alternately spoilt and treated as little adults, capable of looking after themselves. The toy stores alone make you wish you could start over again, especially Pain d'Epices—which is named for the gingerbread that kids adore. It occupies two shopfronts in a 19th-century arcade, but the traditional facade was enhanced around 1930 with art deco etched glass. Every child wants to ride the old-fashioned rocking horse before going inside, where goodies literally hang from the rafters.

PAIN D'EPICES

29 Passage Jouffroy, 9th; 47 70 08 68   *(Mo 12.30pm-7pm; Tu-Sa 10am-7pm)*

Do you like animals? Déyrolle will sell you a stuffed yak ($7,000) and a black swan ($850)—or would you rather have a rat (a bargain at $140)? If in doubt, you could rent several for a week and see which ones seem most at home. You could also have the late lamented Fido stuffed—but this is difficult because pets put on fat, and it's hard to capture their best expressions. Déyrolle was established in 1831 by a naturalist who furnished specimens to schools, and for the past 150 years it has occupied the second floor of a grand

but creaky house of the 1740s. There are trays of beetles, shells, and minerals, but it's the menagerie that keeps the business alive; the stock is replenished from circuses and zoos. This may be the most surreal interior in Paris.

DEYROLLE
46 Rue du Bac, 7th; 42 22 30 07   (Mo-Fr 9am-12.30, 2-6pm; Sa 9am-6pm)

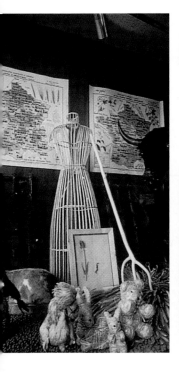  

Every neighborhood once had its *bouchérie* and *boulangérie, poissonérie* and *charcutérie*—which were known to locals and required no further identification. The Pharmacie on the Rue des Francs-Bougeois is a survivor from those simpler times, and has changed very little since the 1820s. The handsome classical facade frames badger-hair shaving brushes and tortoiseshell combs; flasks of blue liquid line the paneled interior with its carved wood beams. Imagine how many little crises have been averted or resolved from behind this counter.

PHARMACIE DES FRANCS-BOURGEOIS

36 Rue des Francs-Bourgeois, 3rd; 48 87 90 59   (Mo 3-8pm; Tu-Fr 10am-8pm; Sa 10.30am-7.30pm; Su 3-7.30pm)

On my first exploration of Parisian shops I chanced on L'Encre Violette in the Marais, just north of the Picasso Museum. I went inside and unexpectedly spent an hour there, sheltering from a downpour, while admiring Monique Toffolon's specialty: phials of purple ink topped with golden sealing wax. I could have bought a poster or a pen, but it was the ink that set the tone. I wrote to tell her I would like to feature her shop in this book and she replied (in the letter reproduced on

the facing page) that it had shut after four years. "The little authentic boutiques that gave certain quarters their charm are closing, one after another," she wrote. "Paris is losing its identity. There you have it—the end of a beautiful and sad story." Cherish and patronize the shops featured here: they represent something precious that is ebbing away: a love of craft, personal service, and a willingness to indulge one's passions.

L'ENCRE VIOLETTE

Monique toffolon.
  ex - Encre Violette –
12, Rue pauline
  94120 Fontenay s/Bois
Tel. 01.48.75.38.93.

Fontenay le 27.05.1998.

Monsieur,

Cela aurait été un immense plaisir de vous recevoir pour parler de "l'encre Violette". mais. voilà, cette boutique ne fait plus partie du paysage parisien.

Après une procédure de quatre années concernant un renouvellement de bail excessif et outrancier, il m'a fallu procéder à une cessation d'activité fin décembre 1997.

Les petits - boutiques authentiques qui font le charme de certains quartiers de Paris ferment les unes après les autres. et toujours pour les mêmes raisons. "un Paris qui perd son identité".

Voici, la fin d'une belle et triste histoire.

Je vous adresse, Monsieur, mes sentiments très distingués.

Addresses, opening hours, nearest metro station

(Opening hours subject to change; most shops close for all or part of August)

Bakeries & patisseries page 12

POILANE, 8 Rue du Cherche-Midi, 6th; 45 48 42 59
   (Mo-Sa 7.15am-8.15pm) Sèvres-Babylone
POUJAURAN, 20 Rue Jean-Nicot, 7th; 47 05 80 88
   (Tu-Sa 8.30am-8.30pm) Latour-Maubourg
STOHRER, 51 Rue Montorgueil, 2nd; 42 33 38 20
   (daily 7.30am-8.30pm) Les Halles

Food & wine page 20

HEDIARD, 21 Place de la Madeleine, 8th; 43 12 88 88
   (Mo-Sa 9.15am-10pm) Madeleine
A LA MERE DE FAMILLE, 35 Rue du Faubourg-Montmartre, 9th; 47 70 83 69
   (Tu-Sa 9.30am-1.30pm, 3-7pm) Le Peletier
BARTHELEMY, 51 Rue de Grenelle, 7th; 45 48 56 75
   (Tu-Sa 8.30am-1pm; 3.30-7.15pm) Rue du Bac
DEBAUVE ET GALLAIS, 30 Rue des Saintes-Pères, 7th; 45 48 54 67
   (Tu-Sa 10am-7pm) Rue du Bac
MARIAGE FRERES, 30-32 Rue du Bourg-Tibourg, 4th; 42 72 28 11
   (Tu-Su 10am-7.30pm) St. Paul
LEGRAND FILLE ET FILS, 1 Rue de la Banque, 2nd; 42 60 07 12
   (Tu-Fr 8.30am-7pm; Sa 8.30am-1pm, 3-7pm) Bourse

Antiques page 34

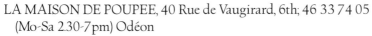

ROBERT CAPIA, 24-26 Galerie Véro-Dodat, 1st; 42 36 25 94
   (Mo-Sa 10am-7pm) Palais-Royal

LA MAISON DE POUPEE, 40 Rue de Vaugirard, 6th; 46 33 74 05
   (Mo-Sa 2.30-7pm) Odéon

LE CABINET DE CURIOSITE, 23 Rue de la Beaune, 7th; 42 61 09 57
   (Mo-Sa 11am-7pm) Rue du Bac

LA GALERIE 34, 34 Passage Jouffroy, 9th; 47 70 89 65
   (Mo-Sa 11.30am-6.30pm) Rue Montmartre

L'HERMINETTE, Le Louvre des Antiquitaires,
   2 Place du Palais-Royal, 1st; 42 61 57 81   (Tu-Sa 11am-7pm) Palais-Royal

AU FOND DE LA COUR, 49 Rue de Seine, 6th; 43 25 81 89
   (Mo-Sa 11am-7pm) Odéon

Collectibles page 50

MADELEINE GELY, 218 Blvd St-Germain, 7th; 42 22 63 35
   (Tu-Su 9.30am-7pm) Rue du Bac

LES DRAPEAUX DE LA FRANCE, 34, 37-38 Galérie Montpensier, 1st;
   40 20 00 11   (Mo-Sa 10am-7pm) Palais-Royal

A MARIE-STUART, 3-5 Galerie Montpensier, 1st; 42 96 28 25
   (Mo-Fr 9am-6.30pm; Sa 9am-noon; 2-6pm) Palais-Royal

THOMAS BOOG, 36 Passage Jouffroy, 9th; 47 70 98 10
   (Mo-Sa 1-7pm) Rue-Montmartre

AISTHESIS, 25 Avenue Daumesnil, 12th; 53 33 00 45
   (Mo-Sa 9am-1pm; 2-6pm; Su 2-6pm) Gare de Lyon

LA TUILE A LOUP, 35 Rue Daubenton, 5th; 47 07 28 90
  (Tu-Sa 10.30am-7.30pm; Su 10.30am-1pm) Censier-Daubenton
PALLADIO, 27 Rue des Saintes-Pères, 6th; 40 15 09 15
  (Mo 2.30-7pm;Tu-Sa 10.30am-7pm) St. Germain des Prés
ENTREE DES ARTISTES, 161 Rue St Martin, 3rd; 48 87 78 58
  (Mo-Sa 11am-7.30pm) Rambuteau
GALERIE URUBAMBA, 4 Rue de la Buchérie, 5th; 43 54 08 24
  (Tu-Sa 2-7.30pm) Maubert-Mutualité
PAPETERIE MODERNE, 12 Rue de la Ferronérie, 1st; 42 36 21 72
  (Mo-Sa 9am-noon, 1-8pm) Les Halles

Printing, books & paper page 70

STERN, 47 Passage des Panoramas, 2nd; 45 08 86 45
  (Mo-Fr 9.30am-12.30pm, 1.30-5.30pm) Rue Montmartre
LIBRAIRIE MONTE CRISTO, 5 Rue de l'Odéon, 6th; 43 26 49 03
  (Tu-Sa 11am-1pm, 2.30-7pm) Odéon
LE PONT TRAVERSEE, 62 Rue de Vaugirard, 6e; 45 48 06 48
  (Tu-Sa noon-7pm) Odéon
MARIE PAPIER, 26 Rue Vavin, 6th; 43 26 46 44
  (Mo-Sa 10am-7pm) Vavin

Decoration & kitchenware page 78

DINERS EN VILLE, 27 Rue deVarenne, 7th; 42 22 78 33
  (Mo 2-7pm; Tu-Sa 11am-7pm) Rue du Bac
VILLA MARAIS, 40 Rue des Francs-Bourgeois, 3rd; 42 78 42 40
  (daily 10.30am-7.30pm) St Paul

MAISON DE FAMILLE, 29 Rue St Sulpice, 6th; 40 46 97 47
(Mo 2.30-7.30pm; Tu-Sa 10.30am-7.30pm) Mabillon

TERRITOIRE, 30 Rue Boissy d'Anglas, 8th; 42 66 22 13
(daily 10.30am-7pm) Madeleine

CIR, 22 Rue St Sulpice, 6th; 43 26 46 50
(Mo 11am-7pm; Tu-Sa 10am-7pm) Mabillon

DEHILLERIN, 18-20 Rue Coquillière, 1st; 42 36 53 13
(Mo-Sa 8am-12.30pm, 2-6pm) Les Halles

Arts & artifice page 90

CHARBONNEL, 13 Quai de Montebello, 5th; 43 54 23 46
(Mo & Sa 10am-5pm; Tu-Fr 9.30am-6pm) Maubert-Mutualité

SENNELIER, 3 Quai Voltaire, 7th; 42 60 72 15
(Mo 9am-noon, 2-6.15pm; Tu-Sa 9am-6.15pm) Rue du Bac

LES CADRES RG, 9 Rue Bonaparte, 6th; 43 26 41 77
(Tu-Sa 9am-noon; 2-6pm) St Germain des Prés

A BRU ET PERRIN, LUTHIERS, 4 rue Elzévir, 4th; 42 77 68 42
(Mo-Sa 9.30am-12.30pm, 2.30-6.30pm) St. Paul

ANDRE BISSONNET, 6 Rue Pas-de-la-Mule, 3rd; 48 87 20 15
(Mo-Sa 2-7pm) St. Paul

EMILIO ROBBA, 29-33 Galérie Vivienne, 2nd; 42 60 43 46
(Mo-Fr 10.30am-7pm; Sa 11am-7pm) Bourse

LES COUTURIERS DE LA NATURE, 23 Rue St Sulpice, 6th; 56 24 06 08
(Mo-Sa 10am-7.30pm) Mabillon

VERTICAL, 63 Avenue Daumesnil, 12th; 43 40 26 26
(Mo-Fr 10am-1pm, 2.30-8pm; Sa 11am-1.30pm, 3-8pm) Gare de Lyons

Wearables page 110

WAREN CREATIONS, 46 Rue du Roi-de-Sicile, 4th; 42 71 16 06
 (Tu, Th, Fr 11.30am-1pm, 2.30-7.30pm; We, Sa 2.30-8pm) St. Paul
MARIE MERCIE, 23 rue St Sulpice, 6th; 43 26 45 83
 (Tu-Sa 11am-7pm) Mabillon
SABBIA ROSA, 71-73 Rue des Saintes-Pères, 6th; 45 48 88 37
 (Mo-Sa 10am-7pm) St. Sulpice
A LA BONNE RENOMEE, 26 Rue Vieille du Temple, 4th; 42 72 03 86
 (Mo-Sa 11am-7pm) St. Paul

Odds & ends page 120

PAIN D'EPICES, 29 Passage Jouffroy, 9th; 47 70 08 68
 (Mo 12.30pm-7pm; Tu-Sa 10am-7pm) Rue Montmartre
DEYROLLE, 46 Rue du Bac, 7th; 42 22 30 07
 (Mo-Fr 9am-12.30, 2-6pm; Sa 9am-6pm) Rue du Bac
PHARMACIE DES FRANCS-BOURGEOIS, 36 Rue des Francs-Bourgeois, 3rd;
 48 87 90 59   (Mo 3-8pm; Tu-Fr 10am-8pm; Sa 10.30am-7.30pm; Su 3-7.30pm) St. Paul

Envoi page 126

L'ENCRE VIOLETTE